VEGETARIAN COOKBOOK

Mouth-Watering, Easy and Healthy Vegetarian Recipes with a 30-Day Diet Plan

AUDREY WILSON

TABLE OF CONTENTS

INTRODUCTION 1
BREAKFAST 2
    01. Silly Scallion Pancakes 2
    02. The Keto Crack Slaw 3
    03. Feisty Grilled Artichokes 4
    04. The Thundering Cinnamon Chocolate Smoothie 5
    05. Vegan Enchilada Macaroni 6
    06. Squash Salad for the Green Lovers! 7
    07. Spinach Scramble 8
    08. Green Eggs 9
    09. Ket-Oats 9
    10. Classic Cheese Soufflés 10
    11. Quick Breakfast Omelet 11
    12. Easy and Tasty Egg Scramble 12
    13. Healthy Breakfast Smoothie 13
    14. Almond Coconut Porridge 14
LUNCH 15
    15. Keto Hummus 15
    16. Mexican-Style Dip 15
    17. Keto Egg Salad 17
    18. Cheesy Vegetable Dip 17
    19. Roasted Green Beans 18
    20. Creamy Cauliflower Spinach Soup 19
    21. Creamy Onion Soup 20
    22. Baked Zucchini Eggplant with Cheese 21
    23. Zucchini Hummus 22
    24. Artichoke Dip 23
    25. Crustless Veggie Quiche 23
    26. Avocado Cilantro Dip 24
DINNER 26
    27. Crispy Broccoli Nuggets 26
    28. Braised Brussels Sprouts 27
    29. Cheesy Stuffed Peppers 27

- 30. Keema Curry 28
- 31. Savory Cake Bites 29
- 32. Spicy Cauliflower Casserole 30
- 33. Cheesy Baked Zucchini 32
- 34. Coconut Cabbage 33
- 35. Tasty Cauliflower Risotto 34
- 36. Healthy Egg Arugula Avocado Salad 35
- 37. Brussel Sprout Salad 36
- 38. Creamy Cauliflower Gratin 36
- 39. Spicy Ginger Lime Broccoli 37
- 40. Fennel Zucchini Pine Nut Salad 38

SNACK 40
- 41. Almond Butter Fudge 40
- 42. White Chocolate Fat Bomb 40
- 43. Brownie Balls 41
- 44. Peanut Butter Fudge 42
- 45. Instant Blueberry Ice Cream 43
- 46. Chia Raspberry Pudding 44
- 47. Choco Mug Brownie 44
- 48. Pistachio Ice Cream 45
- 49. Strawberry Ricotta 46
- 50. No-Bake Raspberry Cheesecake Truffles 47

DESSERT 48
- 51. The Keto Lovers "Magical" Grain Free Granola 48
- 52. Pumpkin Butter Nut Cup 49
- 53. Unique Gingerbread Muffins 50
- 54. The Vegan Pumpkin Spicy Fat Bombs 51
- 55. The Low Carb "Matcha" Bombs 52
- 56. The No-Bake Keto Cheese Cake 53
- 57. Raspberry Chocolate Cups 54
- 58. Exuberant Pumpkin Fudge 55

30-DAY DIET PLAN 56
CONCLUSION 58

DESCRIPTION

You are now well on your way to eating great while fueling your body with the healthy nutrients needed to live a productive and energy charged life! The recipes in this book are all vegetarian-based and delicious. Here, we've covered your whole day, from the time you wake up to midnight snacks. You now have at your disposal everything you need to get started on the path towards a healthier way of living. By reducing or eliminating meat from your diet, you can not only feel better, but you can be confident that you are fueling yourself, family and friends with delicious meals that can bring vibrant health.

Happy Vegetarian Lifestyle!

INTRODUCTION

The vegetarian diet when defined simply is a diet that abstains from the consumption of meat, fish, and fowl flesh. However, being vegetarian covers a wide gamut of categories. There's the vegan where it is simply not just a diet but a type of lifestyle that absolutely embraces not to use any form of animal-sourced items or food in their life—from clothing, shoes, personal items, to food. There is also the lacto-vegetarian who consumes milk even if milk is an animal byproduct. Then the ovo-vegetarian who eats eggs even if it is an animal meat. And then a combination of the last two, the lacto-ovo-vegetarian who includes both milk and eggs in their diet. There are pescatarians who aside from consuming only plant-based foods also eats fish and no other type of meat. And lastly are the vegetarians who abstain from any animal product in their diet alone but still make use of animal products for their clothing—in short, they are one step closer to vegans.

Now it's time to begin frequenting the produce section of your local grocery store – if you haven't already. It will make you healthier in the long run and will enable you to live a more energy filled life. Revisit the first couple chapters of this book to refresh your memory on which foods are the most helpful to you in your pursuit of great plant-based meals. Swap out one unhealthy food item each week that you know is not helping you and put in its place one of the plant-based ingredients that you like. Then have some fun creating the many different recipes in this book. Find out what recipes you like the most so you can make them often and most of all; have some fun exploring all your recipe options.

BREAKFAST

01. Silly Scallion Pancakes

Serving: 4
Preparation Time: 5 minutes
Cook Time: 10 minutes

Ingredients

For Cakes

- ½ a cup of coconut flour
- 2 tablespoon of Psyllium Husk powder
- ½ a teaspoon of garlic powder
- ¼ teaspoon of salt
- 2-3 scallions sliced up into thin portions
- ¼ cup of sesame oil
- 1 cup of warm water

For Sauce

1. 1 tablespoon of tamari sauce
2. 1 teaspoon of rice wine vinegar
3. 1 tablespoon of water
4. 1 teaspoon of sesame oil
5. 1 finely minced garlic clove
6. Chili flakes as needed

Directions:

1. Take a frying pan and place it over medium-low heat
2. Add sesame oil and heat it up
3. Take a mixing bowl and add water, oil, garlic, salt, scallions, warm water and allow it to stand for 5 minutes to allow the flavors to mix up
4. Take another bowl and add coconut flour and the Psyllium Husk

5. Gently add the water to the dry ingredients, making sure to mix it well until the dough forms
6. Separate the dough into individual balls and flatten the balls into 4-inch rounds
7. Place the rounds in your skillet and fry for 5 minutes each side until they are golden
8. Keep repeating until the balls are used up
9. Enjoy!

Nutritional Values:

Calories: 206
Fat: 16g
Carbs: 4g
Protein: 4g

02. The Keto Crack Slaw

Serving: 2
Preparation Time: 5 minutes
Cook Time: 10 minutes

Ingredients

- 4 cups of shredded green cabbage
- ½ a cup of macadamia nuts chopped up
- 1 teaspoon of chili paste
- 1 teaspoon of vinegar
- 2 tablespoon of tamari
- 1 tablespoon of sesame oil
- 2 garlic cloves
- Sesame seeds as needed

Directions:

1. Take a pan and place it over medium-low heat and add tamari, sesame oil, vinegar, sesame oil and chili paste
2. Add your green cabbage

Vegetarian Cookbook

3. Cover and allow it to cook for 5 minutes until the cabbage starts to tender
4. Stir everything and combine them well
5. Add the nuts
6. Cook for 5 minutes more until the nuts are tender
7. Serve and garnish
8. Enjoy!

Nutritional Values:

Calories: 360
Fat: 33g
Carbs: 7g
Protein: 7g

03. Feisty Grilled Artichokes

Preparation Time: 5 minutes
Cooking Time: 30 minute
Serving: 4

Ingredients:

- 2 large sized artichokes
- 1 quartered lemon
- ¾ cup of extra virgin olive oil
- black pepper
- 4 chopped up garlic cloves
- 1 teaspoon of salt
- ½ a teaspoon of ground

Directions:

1. Take a large sized bowl and fill it up with cold water
2. Squeeze a bit of lemon juice from the wedges
3. Trim the upper part of your chokes, making sure to trim any damaged leaves as well
4. Cut the chokes up in half lengthwise portions

5. Add the chokes to your bowl of lemon water
6. Bring the whole pot to a boil
7. Pre-heat your outdoor grill to about medium-high heat
8. Allow the chokes to cook in the boiling pot for 15 minutes
9. Drain the chokes and keep them on the side
10. Take another medium-sized bowl and squeeze the remaining lemon
11. Stir in garlic and olive to the lemon mix
12. Brush up the chokes with the garlic dip and place them on your pre-heated grill
13. Grill for about 10 minutes, making sure to keep basting them until the edges are just slightly charred
14. Serve with the dip and enjoy!

Nutritional Values:

Calories: 402
Fat: 40g
Carbohydrates: 10g
Protein: 2.9g

04. The Thundering Cinnamon Chocolate Smoothie

Serving: 1
Preparation Time: 5 minutes
Cook Time: 0 minutes

Ingredients

- ¾ cup of coconut milk
- ½ of a ripe avocado
- 2 teaspoon of unsweetened cocoa powder
- 1 teaspoon of cinnamon powder
- ¼ teaspoon of vanilla extract
- Stevia as needed
- ½ a teaspoon of

coconut oil

Directions:

1. Add all of the ingredients to your blender and blend well until smooth
2. Allow them it to chill and enjoy!

Nutritional Values:

Calories: 300
Fat: 30g
Carbs: 14g
Protein: 5g

05. Vegan Enchilada Macaroni

Serving: 4
Preparation Time: 20 minutes
Cook Time: 45 minutes

Ingredients

For Sauce

- 1 cup of hemp seeds
- ½ a cup of nutritional yeast
- ¼ cup of sliced red, yellow or orange bell peppers
- ½ a teaspoon of salt
- ½ a teaspoon of onion powder
- ½ a cup of water

For The Main Recipe

- 2 pack of Shirataki macaroni (Tofu)
- 1 can of young, green jackfruit in brine
- ¼ cup of enchilada sauce

Directions:

1. Pre-heat your oven to a temperature of 350 degrees Fahrenheit
2. Drain and chop up your jackfruit with a knife and add 2 tablespoons of enchilada sauce, toss them well.
3. Keep it on the side
4. Blend the sauce ingredients in a blender and process them well
5. Drain and rinse the noodles thoroughly and transfer them to a baking dish
6. Add sauce, jackfruit to the baking dish and mix well
7. Bake for 45 minutes
8. Allow it to cool and enjoy!

Nutritional Values:

Calories: 192
Fat: 7.4g
Carbs: 4.1g
Protein: 9.6g

06. Squash Salad for the Green Lovers!

Preparation Time: 15 minutes
Cooking Time: 30 minutes
Serving: 4

Ingredients:

- 2 tablespoons of extra virgin olive oil
- 1 small sized sliced onion
- 2 medium-sized coarsely chopped tomatoes
- 1 teaspoon of salt
- ¼ teaspoon of pepper
- 2 small zucchini cut up into ½ inch slices
- 2 small sized yellow summer squash cut up into ½ inch slices
- 1 bay leaf
- ½ a teaspoon of dried basil

Directions:

1. Take a skillet and place it over medium heat
2. Add oil and allow it to heat up
3. Add onions and stir-fry them for about 5 minutes
4. Add tomatoes to the pan and mix well
5. Season the mixture with salt and pepper
6. Keep stirring for about 5 minutes until nicely cooked
7. Add bay leaf, zucchini, yellow squash, and basil
8. Lower down the heat and allow it to simmer for about 20 minutes, making sure to keep stirring it occasionally
9. Discard the bay leaf and enjoy!

Nutritional Values:

Calories: 65
Fat:5g
Carbohydrates: 5g
Protein: 1.5g

07. Spinach Scramble

Servings: 1

Ingredients

- ½ cup Spinach (raw)
- 2 tbsp Onions (chopped)
- 1 large Egg
- Dash of Salt
- Dash of Pepper
- ½ tbsp Butter

Directions

1. Heat sauté pan on medium/low heat. Melt butter. Add onions and sauté in pan until translucent.

2. Add spinach and eggs. Gently stir and scramble eggs, add salt and pepper.
3. Remove from heat.

Nutritional Values:

134 calories
Net Carbs: 2.1 g
Total Fat: 10.6 g
Protein: 7 g

08. Green Eggs

Servings: 1

Ingredients

- 2 extra large Eggs
- ½ cup Spinach (raw)
- ½ cup Kale (raw, chopped)
- ½ cup Chard (raw, chopped)
- 1 tsp Coconut oil

Directions

1. Mix eggs and greens in a food processor until smooth.
2. Melt coconut oil in a skillet over medium heat.
3. Pour egg mixture into pan and cook. Scramble eggs to desired doneness and serve immediately.

Nutritional Values:

222 calories
Net Carbs: 3.2 g
Total Fat: 15.6 g
Protein: 16.3 g

09. Ket-Oats

Servings: 1

Ingredients

- 2 tbsp Chia seeds
- 2 tbsp Flaxseed (ground)
- ½ cup Almond milk (unsweetened)
- ⅛ tsp Stevia extract
- ¼ cup Strawberries (sliced)

Directions

1. Combine all ingredients except strawberries in a pot on the stove over medium heat.
2. Bring to a boil, stirring frequently. Remove from heat at desired consistency.
3. Add sliced strawberries and serve hot.

Nutritional Values:

240 calories
Net Carbs: 9 g
Total Fat: 13.7 g
Protein: 7.7 g

10. Classic Cheese Soufflés

Preparation Time: 35 minutes
Serving: 8

Ingredients:

6 large eggs, separated
1/4 tsp cream of tartar

- 1/4 cup chives, chopped
- 2 cups cheddar cheese, shredded
- 3/4 cup heavy cream
- 1/4 tsp cayenne pepper
- 1/2 tsp xanthan gum
- 1/2 tsp pepper
- 1 tsp ground mustard

- 1 tsp salt

Directions:
1. Preheat the oven to 350 F.
2. Spray eight ramekins with cooking spray and place on cookie sheet.
3. In a mixing bowl, whisk together almond flour, cayenne pepper, pepper, mustard, salt, and xanthan gum.
4. Slowly add heavy cream and mix until well combined.
5. Whisk in egg yolks, chives, and cheese until well combined.
6. In a large bowl, add egg whites and cream of tartar and beat until stiff peaks form.
7. Gently fold egg white mixture into the almond flour mixture until well combined.
8. Pour mixture into the prepared ramekins and place on cookie sheet.
9. Bake in preheated oven for 25 minutes or until lightly golden brown.
10. Serve hot and enjoy.

Nutritional Values:

Calories 211
Fat 17 g
Carbohydrates 1 g
Sugar 0.5 g
Protein 12 g
Cholesterol 185 mg

11. Quick Breakfast Omelet

Preparation Time: 15 minutes
Serving: 4

Ingredients:

- 4 large eggs
- 2 tbsp butter
- 2 tbsp olive oil
- 1 tsp herb de

- Provence
- 2 oz cheese
- 10 olives, pitted
- 1/2 tsp salt

Directions:
1. Add eggs, salt, olives, herb de Provence, and olive oil in large bowl and whisk well until frothy.
2. In a large pan, melt butter over medium heat.
3. Pour egg mixture into hot pan and spread evenly.
4. Cover pan with a lid and cook for 3 minutes or until omelet lightly golden brown.
5. Flip omelet to other side and cook for another 2 minutes.
6. Serve hot and enjoy.

Nutritional Values:

Calories 252
Fat 23 g
Carbohydrates 1 g
Sugar 0.5 g
Protein 10 g
Cholesterol 216 mg

12. Easy and Tasty Egg Scramble

Preparation Time: 20 minutes
Serving: 1

Ingredients:

- 3 eggs, lightly beaten
- 1 tbsp coconut oil
- 1/2 cup spinach, chopped
- 1/4 cup bell peppers, chopped
- 4 mushrooms, chopped
- Pepper
- Salt

Directions:
1. Melt 1/2 tablespoon of coconut oil in a pan over medium

heat.
2. Add chopped vegetables to hot pan and sauté.
3. In another pan, melt remaining coconut oil.
4. Once the oil is hot then add eggs and cook over medium heat. Stir frequently to avoid overcooking.
5. Season cooked eggs with pepper and salt.
6. Now add sautéed vegetables in egg and stir well.
7. Serve hot and enjoy.

Nutritional Values:

Calories 335
Fat 27 g
Carbohydrates 6 g
Sugar 3 g
Protein 19 g
Cholesterol 491 mg

13. Healthy Breakfast Smoothie

Preparation Time: 10 minutes
Serving: 6

Ingredients:

- 4 cups water
- 1 tbsp granulated sugar substitute
- 1/2 Hass avocado
- 1/2 cup kiwi
- 1 cup cucumber, peeled and chopped
- 1 tbsp fresh ginger, peeled and chopped
- 2 tbsp fresh parsley
- 1/3 cup pineapple, chopped
- 1 cup romaine lettuce

Directions:

1. Add all ingredients into the blender and blend until smooth.
2. Pour into the glass and serve.

Nutritional Values:

Calories 53
Fat 3 g
Carbohydrates 6 g
Sugar 2 g
Protein 0.9 g
Cholesterol 0 mg

14. Almond Coconut Porridge

Preparation Time: 15 minutes
Serving: 2

Ingredients:

- 3/4 cup coconut cream
- 1/2 cup ground almonds
- 1/8 tsp cardamom
- 1/8 tsp nutmeg
- 1/8 tsp cloves
- 1 tsp stevia
- 1 tsp ground cinnamon

Directions:

1. Add coconut cream in small saucepan and heat over medium heat until it forms a liquid.
2. Add stevia and ground almonds and stir well to combine.
3. Stir well for 5 minutes then add cinnamon, cloves, nutmeg and cardamom. Stir well.
4. Serve hot and enjoy.

Nutritional Values:

Calories 349
Fat 33 g
Carbohydrates 11 g
Sugar 4 g
Protein 7 g
Cholesterol 0 mg

LUNCH

15. Keto Hummus

Servings: 6
Preparation Time: About 20 minutes

Ingredients:

- 3 cups cauliflower florets
- 2 Tbsp. water
- 2 Tbsp. olive oil
- ½ tsp. salt
- 3 cloves garlic
- 1 ½ Tbsp. tahini paste
- 3 Tbsp. fresh lemon juice
- 3 additional Tbsp. olive oil
- ¾ tsp. kosher salt

Directions:
1. Add the cauliflower, water, olive oil, salt, and garlic cloves to a microwave safe dish. Microwave for about 15 minutes until cauliflower is soft.
2. Transfer the mixture to a blender or food processor and blend until it's smooth. Add the tahini, lemon juice, additional olive oil, and kosher salt. Blend until smooth.

Nutritional Values:

Total Fat: 14 g
Carbohydrates: 4 g
Protein: 2 g

16. Mexican-Style Dip

Servings: 16
Preparation Time: About 35 minutes

Ingredients:

- 4 cups cauliflower florets, cooked and

- drained
- 2 Tbsp. mayonnaise
- 1 tsp. Cajun seasoning
- 3 Tbsp. heavy whipping cream
- ½ tsp. ground cumin
- 3 Tbsp. canned chipotle
- 1 Tbsp. olive oil
- 2 cups avocado, mashed
- 2 tsp. fresh lime juice
- ½ tsp. kosher salt
- ¼ tsp. ground black pepper
- 2 cups sour cream
- 1 cup tomatoes, chopped
- 1 cup cheddar cheese, shredded
- ½ cup scallions, chopped
- ¼ cup black olives, sliced

Directions:

1. Combine the cooked cauliflower, mayonnaise, Cajun seasoning, heavy whipping cream, cumin, chipotle, and oil in a blender or food processor.
2. Blend until smooth.
3. Mash the avocados with a fork, leaving them slightly chunky
4. Stir in the lime juice, salt and pepper.
5. Spread the cauliflower layer evenly over the bottom of a casserole dish.
6. Spread the sour cream over the cauliflower.
7. Spoon the avocado on top of the sour cream and gently spread it out to form a layer on top of the sour cream.
8. Sprinkle the chopped tomatoes over the avocado.
9. Spread the shredded cheese over the tomatoes, followed by the scallions.
10. Finally, evenly sprinkle the olives on top.
11. Can be stored in the refrigerator for up to five days.

Nutritional Values:

Total Fat: 15 g
Carbohydrates: 6 g

Protein: 4 g

17. Keto Egg Salad

Servings: 8-10
Preparation Time: About 25 minutes

Ingredients:

- 10 eggs
- 2 Tbsp. mayonnaise
- 1 tsp. Dijon mustard
- ¼ tsp. smoked paprika
- 1 spring onion, diced
- Salt and pepper to taste

Directions:

1. Place the eggs in a large pot covered with an inch of cold water. Bring the water to a boil and boil the eggs for 8-10 minutes. Remove them and cool them quickly in cold water.
2. Shell the eggs and transfer them to a cutting board. Chop the eggs coarsely and transfer to a mixing bowl.
3. Add the rest of the ingredients to the mixing bowl toss well to combine.
4. Serve garnished with chopped chives.

Nutritional Values:

Total Fat: 26 g
Carbohydrates: 2 g
Protein: 16 g

18. Cheesy Vegetable Dip

Servings: 6
Preparation Time: About 35 minutes

Ingredients:

- 1 can (14 oz.) hearts of palm, drained

- 3 green onions, chopped
- ¼ cup mayonnaise
- 2 Tbsp. Italian seasoning
- ½ cup Parmesan cheese, grated
- 2 large eggs

Directions:

1. Pre-heat oven to 350 degrees Fahrenheit.
2. Lightly coat a small baking dish with cooking oil spray
3. Add all the ingredients, excluding the eggs, to a food processor and pulse until the mixture is well-combined but still slightly chunky.
4. Add the eggs and pulse again briefly, just enough to combine.
5. Spoon the dip into the baking dish and bake for 15-20 minutes, until the dip is starting to bubble.
6. Carefully stir the dip and sprinkle the top with a bit more Parmesan cheese.
7. Return to the oven and bake until the top is beginning to brown, about 10 minutes.

Nutritional Values:

Total Fat: 9 g
Carbohydrates: 3 g
Protein: 5 g

19. Roasted Green Beans

Preparation Time: 15 minutes
Cook time: 30 minutes
Servings: 4

Ingredients:

- 1 lb. green beans, frozen
- 2 tablespoons extra-virgin olive oil
- ½ teaspoon onion powder
- ½ teaspoon garlic powder

Lunch

- ½ teaspoon sea salt
- ½ teaspoon pepper

Directions:

1. Preheat your oven to 425°Fahrenheit. Spray a cooking tray with cooking spray. In a bowl add all your ingredients and mix well.
2. Spread the green beans on the prepared baking tray and bake for 30 minutes. Serve and enjoy!

Nutritional Values:

Calories: 98
Sugar: 1.8 g
Carbohydrates: 8.8 g
Fat: 7.2 g
Cholesterol: 0 mg
Protein: 2.2 g

20. Creamy Cauliflower Spinach Soup

Preparation Time: 10 minutes
Cook time: 35 minutes
Servings: 5

Ingredients:

- 5 watercress, chopped
- 8 cups vegetable broth
- 1 lb. cauliflower, chopped
- 5-ounces spinach, fresh, chopped
- ½ cup coconut milk
- Sea salt

Directions:

1. Add cauliflower along with broth to a large pot over medium heat for 15 minutes, bring to a boil.
2. Add spinach and watercress, cook for another 10 minutes. Remove from heat and using a blender puree the soup until smooth.

3. Add coconut milk and stir well. Season with sea salt. Serve hot and enjoy!

Nutritional Values:

Calories: 153
Cholesterol: 0 mg
Sugar: 4.3 g
Fat: 8.3 g
Carbohydrates: 8.7 g
Protein: 11.9 g

21. Creamy Onion Soup

Preparation Time: 15 minutes
Cook time: 25 minutes
Servings: 4

Ingredients:

- 1 shallot, sliced
- Sea salt
- 1 ½ tablespoons extra-virgin olive oil
- 1 leek, sliced
- 1 garlic clove, chopped
- 4 cups vegetable stock
- 1 onion, sliced

Directions:

1. Add the olive oil and vegetable stock into a large saucepan over medium heat, bring to a boil.
2. Add the remaining ingredients and stir. Cover and simmer for 25 minutes. Puree your soup using a blender until smooth.
3. Serve warm and enjoy!

Nutritional Values:

Calories: 90
Sugar: 4.1 g

Fat: 7.4 g
Carbohydrates: 10.1 g
Cholesterol: 0 mg
Protein: 1 g

22. Baked Zucchini Eggplant with Cheese

Preparation Time: 15 minutes
Cook time: 35 minutes
Servings: 6

Ingredients:

- 3-ounces Parmesan cheese, grated
- 3 medium zucchinis, sliced
- 1 tablespoon extra-virgin olive oil
- 1 medium eggplant, sliced
- 1 cup cherry tomatoes, halved
- ¼ cup parsley, chopped
- ¼ cup basil, chopped
- 4 garlic cloves, minced
- ¼ teaspoon sea salt
- ¼ teaspoon pepper
- Directions:
- Preheat your oven to
- e and enjoy!

350°Fahrenheit. Spray a baking dish with cooking spray.

- In a mixing bowl, add eggplant, cherry tomatoes, zucchini, olive oil, cheese, basil, garlic, salt, and pepper, toss to mix.
- Transfer eggplant mixture to baking dish and place into preheated oven to bake for 35 minutes.
- Garnish with chopped parsley. Serv

Nutritional Values:

Calories: 110
Cholesterol: 10 mg

Carbohydrates: 10.4 g
Fat: 5.8 g

Sugar: 4.8 g

Protein: 7 g

23. Zucchini Hummus

Preparation Time: 10 minutes
Cook time: 10 minutes
Servings: 4

Ingredients:

- 3 garlic cloves
- 4 zucchinis, halved
- 3 tablespoons tahini
- 1 tablespoon extra-virgin olive oil
- 1 tablespoon lemon juice, fresh
- 1 teaspoon cumin
- ¼ cup cilantro, chopped
- Pepper and salt to taste

Directions:

1. Place your zucchini onto the grill. Season zucchini with salt and pepper. Grill for 10 minutes.
2. Add grilled zucchini, lemon juice, cilantro, cumin, tahini, garlic, olive oil, salt, and pepper into a blender and blend until smooth.
3. Pour the zucchini mixture into serving bowl. Sprinkle top with paprika.
4. Serve and enjoy!

Nutritional Values:

Calories: 138
Cholesterol: 0 mg
Sugar: 4.9 g
Fat: 10.1 g
Carbohydrates: 11.1 g
Protein: 4.6 g

24. Artichoke Dip

Preparation Time: 5 minutes
Cook time: 35 minutes
Servings: 4

Ingredients:

- 15-ounces artichoke hearts, drained
- 1 cup cheddar cheese, shredded
- 3 cups arugula, chopped
- 1 teaspoon Worcestershire sauce
- ½ cup mayonnaise
- 1 tablespoon onion, minced

Directions:

1. Preheat your oven to 350°Fahrenheit. Blend all ingredients using a blender and blend until smooth.
2. Pour artichoke mixture into a baking dish and bake in preheated oven for 30 minutes.
3. Serve with crackers and enjoy!

Nutritional Values:

Calories: 284
Fat: 19.4 g
Cholesterol: 37 mg
Sugar: 3.8 g
Carbohydrates: 19 g
Protein: 11.2 g

25. Crustless Veggie Quiche

Preparation Time: 10 minutes
Cook time: 30 minutes
Servings: 6

Ingredients:

- 1 cup milk
- 1 cup tomatoes, chopped
- 1 cup Parmesan cheese, grated, fresh
- 1 onion, chopped
- 1 cup zucchini, chopped
- 8 eggs, organic
- ½ teaspoon pepper
- 1 teaspoon sea salt

Directions:

1. Preheat your oven to 400°Fahrenheit. In a pan placed over medium heat, melt butter, add onion and sauté until lightly brown.
2. Add zucchini and tomatoes to pan and sauté for 5 minutes. Beat eggs with milk, cheese, pepper and salt in a bowl.
3. Pour egg mixture over veggies and bake in preheated oven for 30 minutes.
4. Allow dish to cool for 10 minutes, cut into slices, serve and enjoy!

Nutritional Values:

Calories: 257
Sugar: 4.2 g
Fat: 16.7 g
Carbohydrates: 8.1 g
Cholesterol: 257 mg
Protein: 21.4 g

26. Avocado Cilantro Dip

Preparation Time: 10 minutes
Servings: 2

Ingredients:

Lunch

- 1 cup cilantro, fresh
- 1 garlic clove
- ½ cup sour cream
- ½ teaspoon onion powder
- 1 fresh lemon juice
- 2 avocados
- ¼ teaspoon sea salt

Directions:
1. Using your blender blend ingredients, and blend until smooth.
2. Place the mixture in your fridge to combine flavors for a few hours.
3. Serve with crackers and enjoy!

Nutritional Values:

Calories: 273
Cholesterol: 13 mg
Sugar: 2.1 g
Fat: 25.7 g
Carbohydrates: 11.6 g
Protein: 3 g

DINNER

27. Crispy Broccoli Nuggets

Servings: 4-6
Preparation Time: About 25 minutes

Ingredients:

- ¾ cup almond flour
- 7 Tbsp. flaxseed meal
- 4 oz. fresh broccoli
- 4 oz. mozzarella cheese
- 2 large eggs
- 2 tsp. baking powder
- Salt and pepper to taste
- ¼ cup mayonnaise
- ¼ cup fresh chopped dill
- ½ Tbsp. lemon juice

Directions:

1. Add broccoli to a food processor and pulse until the broccoli is ground to a meal-like consistency.
2. Combine the cheese, almond flour, flaxseed meal and baking powder with the broccoli in a large mixing bowl.
3. Add the eggs and mix well. to form a thick batter
4. Form the batter into 1-inch balls and dredge in flax seed meal.
5. Heat cooking oil in a fryer or deep skillet to 375 degrees Fahrenheit.
6. Fry the nuggets until they're golden brown, turning once to brown both side. This should take 3-5 minutes.
7. Serve hot.

Nutritional Values:

Total Fat: 8 g
Carbohydrates: 2 g
Protein: 5 g

28. Braised Brussels Sprouts

Servings: 4-6
Preparation Time: About 25 minutes

Ingredients:

- 4 cups Brussels sprouts, ends trimmed and cut in half
- 1 tsp. olive oil
- ½ cup water
- Salt to taste

Directions:

1. Heat the oil over medium-high heat in a heavy skillet. When the oil is hot, sauté the Brussels sprouts, stirring frequently, until the sprouts are beginning to brown and get crisp at the edges. This should take about 5 minutes.
2. When the sprouts are browned, carefully add the water to the pot.
3. Cover and simmer until the sprouts are tender, about 15 minutes.
4. Remove the cover and season the Brussels sprout with sea salt to taste.
5. Serve hot.

Nutritional Values:

Total Fat: 1 gram
Carbohydrates: 8 g
Protein: 3 g

29. Cheesy Stuffed Peppers

Servings: 2
Preparation Time: About 60 minutes

Ingredients:

- 2 medium bell peppers
- 4 large eggs
- ½ cup ricotta cheese
- ½ cup shredded mozzarella
- ½ cup grated Parmesan cheese
- 1 tsp. garlic powder
- ¼ tsp. dried parsley
- ¼ cup baby spinach
- 2 Tbsp. Parmesan cheese for topping

Directions:

1. Pre-heat oven to 375 degrees Fahrenheit.
2. Slice the peppers in half vertically and remove the seeds.
3. Combine the cheeses, eggs, garlic powder, and parsley in a food processor and pulse until combined and smooth.
4. Spoon the egg mixture into each pepper half, stopping just below the edge. Carefully add baby spinach leaves, stirring to cover them with the egg mixture.
5. Cover the peppers with foil and bake for 35-45 minutes. The egg should be set and firm at this point.
6. Top with Parmesan cheese and place under a hot broiler for 3-5 minutes until the cheese begins to brown.

Nutritional Values:

Total Fat: 16 g
Carbohydrates: 6 g
Protein: 18 g

30. Keema Curry

Servings: 4-6
Preparation Time: About 30 minutes

Ingredients:

- 2 Tbsp. olive oil
- 1 onion, diced
- 4 cloves garlic, minced
- 1 inch piece of fresh ginger, peeled and minced
- 1 Serrano pepper,

- seeded and minced
- 1 Tbsp. coriander
- 1 tsp. paprika
- 1 tsp. salt
- ½ tsp. turmeric
- ½ tsp. black pepper
- ½ tsp. garam masala
- ½ tsp. cumin powder
- ¼ teaspoon cayenne
- ¼ tsp. ground cardamom
- 1 can diced tomatoes
- 2 cups fresh or frozen peas

Directions:

1. Heat the oil over medium-high heat in a large skillet. When the oil is hot, sauté the onions until they are beginning to brown, about 8 minutes.
2. Add garlic, ginger, Serrano pepper, and spices, and sauté for about 1 minute more.
3. Add the tomatoes and peas to the pan, stirring to combine all the ingredients.
4. Simmer until the spices are fragrant and the sauce is bubbly, about 15 minutes.
5. Serve the curry hot.

Nutritional Values:

Total Fat: 20 g
Carbohydrates: 17 g
Protein: 30 g

31. Savory Cake Bites

Servings: 1
Preparation Time: About 10 minutes

Ingredients:

- 1 large egg
- 2 Tbsp. butter
- 2 Tbsp. almond flour
- ½ tsp. baking powder
- 5 tsp. sun dried tomato pesto

- 1 Tbsp. almond flour
- Salt to taste

Directions:

1. Combine all ingredients in a small mixing bowl and mix well.
2. Pour mixture into a microwave-safe mug.
3. Microwave on high for about 90 seconds.
4. Remove the mug from the microwave and allow to cool slightly.
5. Gently slip the cake out of the mug and serve warm.

Nutritional Values:

Total Fat: 40 g
Carbohydrates: 5 g
Protein: 12 g

32. Spicy Cauliflower Casserole

Servings: 6
Preparation Time: About 40 minutes

Ingredients:

For filling:

- 1
- head of cauliflower
- 2 Tbsp. heavy cream
- 1 Tbsp. butter
- ¼ cup sharp cheddar cheese, shredded
- 1 Tbsp. raw jalapenos, seeded and chopped
- ¼ tsp. garlic powder
- Salt and pepper to taste

For middle layer:

- 6 oz. cream cheese, softened
- ½ cup cheddar cheese, shredded
- ¼ cup salsa verde
- For topping:
- ¾ cup colby jack cheese, shredded

- ¼ cup raw jalapenos, sliced and seeded

Directions:

1. Pre-heat oven to 375 degrees Fahrenheit.
2. Core and cut the cauliflower into bite-sized pieces. Place the cauliflower into a microwave-safe bowl with cream and butter. Microwave, uncovered, on high for 10 minutes. Stir well and then microwave for another 6-8 minutes.
3. Transfer the cauliflower to a blender or food processor and add cheese, jalapenos, and garlic powder. Process until the mixture is smooth, and season with salt and pepper to taste.
4. In a microwave-safe bowl, microwave the cream cheese for 30 seconds. Stir in the shredded cheese and salsa verde.
5. Spread the cauliflower puree in the bottom of a medium-size baking dish. Spread a layer of the cream cheese mixture on top of the cauliflower. Top with a layer of colby jack cheese and jalapeno slices.
6. Place in the oven and bake for 20 minutes.
7. Serve hot.

Nutritional Values:

Total Fat: 29 g
Carbohydrates: 4 g
Protein: 13 g

33. Cheesy Baked Zucchini

Servings: 9
Preparation Time: About 60 minutes

Ingredients:

- 4 cups sliced zucchini
- 1 small onion, peeled and sliced thin
- Salt and pepper to taste
- 1 ½ cups pepper jack cheese, shredded
- 2 Tbsp. butter
- ½ tsp. garlic powder
- ½ cup heavy whipping cream

Directions:

1. Preheat oven to 375 degrees Fahrenheit.
2. Layer a third of the sliced zucchini and onion in the bottom of a greased baking dish. Season with salt and pepper.
3. Layer ½ cup of cheese over the zucchini.
4. Repeat these steps twice with the rest of the zucchini, onion and cheese to make three layers.
5. Combine the garlic powder, butter, and heavy cream in a microwave-safe dish. Microwave for 1 minute to melt the butter and then stir well.
6. Pour the butter mixture over the vegetable and cheese in the baking dish.
7. Bake for about 45 minutes until the casserole is beginning to brown on top.
8. Serve warm.

Nutritional Values:

Total Fat: 20 g
Carbohydrates: 3 g
Protein: 8 g

34. Coconut Cabbage

Servings: 4-6
Preparation Time: About 25 minutes

Ingredients:

- 1 Tbsp. olive oil
- 1 medium onion, sliced
- 1 tsp. salt
- 2 cloves garlic, minced
- ½ Thai red chili, seeded and sliced
- 1 tsp. dry mustard
- 1 Tbsp. curry powder
- 1 Tbsp. turmeric powder
- 1 Asian cabbage, cored and shredded
- 1 carrot, peeled and sliced
- 2 lemon juice
- ½ cup dried unsweetened coconut, shredded
- 1/3 cup water

Directions:

1. Heat the oil in a large skillet over medium-high heat. When the oil is hot, sauté the onions until they are soft and translucent, about 5 minutes.
2. Add garlic, chili pepper and spices and sauté for about 30 seconds more, just until fragrant.
3. Add the cabbage, carrot, lemon juice and water, stirring to combine.
4. Simmer until the vegetable are tender, about 15 minutes.
5. Remove the cover and serve the cabbage hot as a side dish.

Nutritional Values:

Total Fat: 1 gram
Carbohydrates: 6 g
Protein: 1 gram

35. Tasty Cauliflower Risotto

Preparation Time: 20 minutes
Serving: 4

Ingredients:

- 1 medium cauliflower
- 3 tbsp chives, chopped
- 1 cup parmesan cheese, grated
- 1 cup cheddar cheese, shredded
- 1 tsp Dijon mustard
- 1 cup vegetable stock
- 1 small onion, chopped
- 4 tbsp butter
- Salt

Directions:

1. Cut the stem of cauliflower and cut cauliflower in half.
2. Add cauliflower in food processor and process until it looks like rice.
3. Melt butter in a pan over medium heat.
4. Add onion to the pan and sauté until lightly brown.
5. Add cauliflower rice in the pan and stir well to combine.
6. Pour vegetable stock into the pan and cook for 5 minutes.
7. Add mustard and stir well.
8. Add parmesan cheese and cheddar cheese and stir until cheese melted.
9. Garnish with chopped chives.
10. Serve hot and enjoy.

Nutritional Values:

Calories 363
Fat 27 g
Carbohydrates 10 g
Sugar 4 g
Protein 18 g
Cholesterol 80 mg

36. Healthy Egg Arugula Avocado Salad

Preparation Time: 20 minutes
Serving: 2

Ingredients:

- 4 large eggs, hard-boiled, peel and chopped
- 2 tsp Dijon mustard
- 2 garlic cloves, minced
- 1/2 cup sour cream
- 4 cups arugula
- 1 large avocado, peel and sliced
- Pepper
- Salt

Directions:

1. For dressing: In a bowl combine together Dijon mustard, garlic, sour cream, pepper, and salt.
2. Add eggs, arugula, and avocado in a large bowl and toss well.
3. Now add dressing and mix well.
4. Serve and enjoy.

Nutritional Values:

Calories 489
Fat 42 g
Carbohydrates 13 g
Sugar 2 g
Protein 17 g
Cholesterol 397 mg

Vegetarian Cookbook

37. Brussel Sprout Salad

Preparation Time: 10 minutes
Serving: 1

Ingredients:

- 6 Brussels sprouts, cut in half lengthwise
- 1 tbsp parmesan cheese, grated
- 1 tsp olive oil
- 1/2 tsp apple cider vinegar
- 1/4 tsp pepper
- 1/4 tsp salt

Directions:

1. Add all ingredients to the bowl and toss well.
2. Serve and enjoy.

Nutritional Values:

Calories 111
Fat 6 g
Carbohydrates 10 g
Sugar 2 g
Protein 6 g
Cholesterol 5 mg

38. Creamy Cauliflower Gratin

Preparation Time: 35 minutes
Serving: 4

Ingredients:

- 4 cups cauliflower florets
- 6 pepper jack cheese slices

- 1/3 cup heavy whipping cream
- 4 tbsp butter
- Pepper
- Salt

Directions:

1. Add cauliflower florets, pepper, salt, heavy whipping cream and butter in microwave safe dish.
2. Place dish in oven and microwave for 25 minutes.
3. Using fork slightly mash the cauliflower florets.
4. Place cheese slices over cauliflower mixture and microwave for 2 minutes or until cheese melted.
5. Serve warm and enjoy.

Nutritional Values:

Calories 326
Fat 28 g
Carbohydrates 5 g
Sugar 2 g
Protein 11 g
Cholesterol 80 mg

39. Spicy Ginger Lime Broccoli

Preparation Time: 20 minutes
Serving: 4

Ingredients:

- 2 small broccoli, cut into florets
- 8 tbsp olive oil
- 1 fresh lime juice
- 4 garlic cloves, minced
- 2 tbsp fresh ginger, grated

- 2 tsp fresh chili pepper, chopped

Directions:

1. Place broccoli florets into the steamer and steamer for 8 minutes or until tender.
2. In a small bowl, combine together chili pepper, ginger, garlic, lime juice and olive oil.
3. Place steamed broccoli on serving dish then pour bowl mixture over broccoli.
4. Serve and enjoy.

Nutritional Values:

Calories 293
Fat 28 g
Carbohydrates 8 g
Sugar 1 g
Protein 1 g
Cholesterol 0 mg

40. Fennel Zucchini Pine Nut Salad

Preparation Time: 15 minutes
Serving: 4

Ingredients:

- 2 tbsp pine nuts, toasted
- 2 small fennel, sliced
- 2 tsp fresh dill, chopped
- 1/2 orange juice
- 4 tbsp extra virgin olive oil
- 1 cup green leaf lettuce, chopped
- 1 cup arugula
- 2 small zucchini, sliced

- 1/2 tsp salt

Directions:

1. In a small bowl, combine together olive oil, salt, and orange juice.
2. Add all ingredients into the large bowl and mix well.
3. Now pour olive oil mixture over salad and toss well.
4. Serve and enjoy.

Nutritional Values:

Calories 204
Fat 17 g
Carbohydrates 13 g
Sugar 2 g
Protein 3 g
Cholesterol 0 mg

SNACK

41. Almond Butter Fudge

Preparation Time: 15 minutes
Cook time: 2 minutes
Servings: 8

Ingredients:

- 2 ½ tablespoons coconut oil
- 2 ½ tablespoons honey
- ½ cup almond butter

Directions:

1. Combine coconut oil and almond butter in a saucepan and warm for 2 minutes or until melted.
2. Add honey and stir. Pour the mixture into candy container and store in the fridge until set. Serve and enjoy!

Nutritional Values:

Calories: 63
Carbohydrates: 5.6 g
Fat: 4.8 g
Sugars: 5.4 g
Cholesterol: 0 mg
Protein: 0.2 g

42. White Chocolate Fat Bomb

Preparation Time: 5 minutes
Cook time: 2 minutes
Servings: 8

Ingredients:

- 4 tablespoons butter
- 4 tablespoons coconut oil
- 4 tablespoons erythritol, powdered
- 4-ounces cocoa butter
- ¼ teaspoon salt
- ¼ teaspoon Stevia
- ½ teaspoon vanilla extract
- ½ cup walnuts, chopped

Directions:

1. Add your cocoa butter and coconut oil into a pan over medium heat for 2 minutes or until melted, then remove from heat.
2. Add Stevia, vanilla extract, erythritol, salt, and walnuts. Mix well to combine.
3. Pour mixture into silicone mold and place in the fridge for an hour.
4. Serve and enjoy!

Nutritional Values:

Calories: 265
Fat: 20.2 g
Carbohydrates: 0.8 g
Protein: 0.9 g
Fiber: 0.5
Cholesterol: 15 mg

43. Brownie Balls

Preparation Time: 20 minutes
Servings: 12

Ingredients:

- 6 dates, pitted
- ¼ cup chocolate chips
- ½ cup almond meal

- 2 tablespoons coconut butter
- 2 teaspoons vanilla extract

Directions:

1. Add your dates to your food processor and pulse for 3 minutes. Add all remaining ingredients except chocolate chips.
2. Pulse until well combined. Add chocolate chips and pulse for 2 times.
3. Form dough into 12 balls and place into the fridge for 1 hour.
4. Serve and enjoy!

Nutritional Values:

Calories: 80
Fat: 6 g
Cholesterol: 1 mg
Carbohydrates: 7.3 g
Protein: 1.5 g

44. Peanut Butter Fudge

Preparation Time: 15 minutes
Cook time: 2 minutes
Servings: 20

Ingredients:

- 12-ounces peanut butter, smooth
- 4 tablespoons maple syrup
- 4 tablespoons coconut cream
- 3 tablespoons coconut oil
- Pinch of salt

Directions:

1. Line baking tray with parchment paper. Melt the coconut and maple syrup in a pan over low heat for about 2 minutes or until melted.
2. Add peanut butter, coconut cream, and salt into the pan, stir well. Pour fudge mixture into the prepared baking dish and place in the fridge for an hour.
3. Cut into pieces serve and enjoy!

Nutritional Values:

Calories: 135
Carbohydrates: 6.2 g
Sugar: 4.1 g
Cholesterol: 0 mg
Fat: 11.3 g
Protein: 4.3 g

45. Instant Blueberry Ice Cream

Preparation Time: 15 minutes
Servings: 2

Ingredients:

- 1 cup blueberries
- 1 teaspoon lemon juice, fresh
- 1 tablespoon Splenda
- ½ cup heavy cream

Directions:

1. Add all ingredients into a blender and blend until smooth. Serve immediately and enjoy!

Nutritional Values:

Calories: 176
Carbohydrates: 17.4 g

Vegetarian Cookbook

Sugar: 13.3 g
Cholesterol: 41 mg
Fat: 11.4 g
Protein: 1.2 g

46. Chia Raspberry Pudding

Preparation Time: 3 hours and 10 minutes
Servings: 2

Ingredients:

- 4 tablespoons chia seeds
- ½ cup raspberries
- 1 cup coconut milk

Directions:

2. Add the raspberry and coconut milk into your blender and blend until smooth. Pour the mixture into a mason jar. Add chia seeds and stir. Cap jar and shake. Place in the fridge for 3 hours then serve and enjoy!

Nutritional Values:

Calories: 408
Fat: 38.8 g
Sugar: 5.4 g
Carbohydrates: 22.3 g
Cholesterol: 0 mg
Protein: 9.1 g

47. Choco Mug Brownie

Preparation Time: 5 minutes
Cook time: 30 seconds
Servings: 1

Snack

Ingredients:

- ½ teaspoon baking powder
- ¼ cup almond milk
- 1 scoop chocolate protein powder
- 1 tablespoon cocoa powder

Directions:

3. In a safe microwave, mug blend the protein powder, cocoa, and baking powder.
4. Add milk in mug and stir. Place the mug in the microwave for 30 seconds. Enjoy!

Nutritional Values:

Calories: 207
Carbohydrates: 9.5 g
Fat: 15.8 g
Sugar: 3.1 g
Cholesterol: 20 mg
Protein: 12.4 g

48. Pistachio Ice Cream

Preparation Time: 20 minutes
Cook time: 3 minutes
Servings: 3

Ingredients:

- 2 egg yolks, organic
- 1 ¾ cups coconut milk
- 1 tablespoon oil
- 1 tablespoon honey
- 5 tablespoons pistachio nuts, chopped
- 1 teaspoon vanilla

Directions:

1. In a bowl, add honey, egg yolks, oil, coconut milk, salt, and whisk.
2. Place the mixture into the fridge for an hour. In a pan over medium heat roast chopped pistachio nuts.
3. Run ice cream mixture in ice cream maker and add in the roasted pistachios halfway through.
4. Serve chilled and enjoy!

Nutritional Values:

Calories: 457
Carbohydrates: 15.8 g
Fat: 43.8 g

Sugar: 11.1 g
Cholesterol: 140 mg
Protein: 6.3 g

49. Strawberry Ricotta

Preparation Time: 10 minutes
Servings: 2

Ingredients:

- 2 teaspoon Splenda
- 1 cup strawberries, washed, sliced
- ½ cup ricotta cheese

Directions:

1. Add ricotta cheese to a shallow serving dish. Sprinkle with Splenda. Mash strawberries and pour over ricotta. Serve and enjoy!

Nutritional Values:

Calories: 129
Carbohydrates: 12.7 g
Fat: 5.1 g

Sugar: 7.7 g
Cholesterol: 19 mg
Protein: 7.5 g

Snack

50. No-Bake Raspberry Cheesecake Truffles

Preparation Time: 3 hours
Servings: 48 (truffles)

Ingredients:

- ½ cup erythritol, powdered
- 8-ounces cream cheese softened
- 1 teaspoon vanilla Stevia
- Pinch of salt
- 1 ½ cups sugar-free chocolate chips, melted
- ¼ cup coconut oil, melted
- Few drops of natural red food coloring
- 3 teaspoons raspberry extract
- 2 tablespoons heavy cream

Directions:

2. In a stand mixer blend erythritol and cream cheese until smooth.
3. Add the Stevia, cream, raspberry extract, salt, natural red food coloring and mix well. Slowly add in the coconut oil and continue to blend on high until it is incorporated.
4. Scrape down the sides of the bowl to make sure it is all mixed well. Place in fridge for 1 hour.
5. On a parchment-lined baking sheet scoop out the batter using a 1 ¼ inch mini cookie scoop. Should make 48 balls.
6. Freeze for 1 hour before coating with melted chocolate. Drop one cheesecake truffle into chocolate at a time and place back on the lined baking pan.
7. Place in fridge for 1 hour.
8. Serve and enjoy!

DESSERT

51. The Keto Lovers "Magical" Grain Free Granola

Serving: 10
Preparation Time: 10 minutes
Cook Time: 75 minutes

Ingredients

- ½ a cup of raw sunflower seeds
- ½ a cup of raw hemp hearts
- ½ a cup of flaxseeds
- ¼ cup of chia seeds
- 2 tablespoon of Psyllium Husk powder
- 1 tablespoon of cinnamon
- Stevia
- ½ a teaspoon of baking powder
- ½ a teaspoon of salt
- 1 cup of water

Directions:

1. Pre-heat your oven to 300 degrees Fahrenheit
2. Line up a baking sheet with parchment paper
3. Take your food processor and grind all the seeds
4. Add the dry ingredients and mix well
5. Stir in water until fully incorporated
6. Allow the mixture to sit for a while until it thickens up
7. Spread the mixture evenly on top of your baking sheet (giving a thickness of about ¼ inch)
8. Bake for 45 minutes
9. Break apart the granola and keep baking for another 30 minutes until the pieces are crunchy
10. Remove and allow them to cool
11. Enjoy!

Dessert

Nutritional Values:

Calories: 292
Fat: 25g
Carbs: 12g
Protein: 8g

52. Pumpkin Butter Nut Cup

Serves: 5
Preparation Time: 135 minutes
Cook Time: 0 minute

For Filing

- ½ a cup of organic pumpkin puree
- 1/2a cup of almond butter
- 4 tablespoon of organic coconut oil
- ¼ teaspoon of organic ground nutmeg
- ¼ teaspoon of organic ground ginger
- 1 teaspoon of organic ground cinnamon
- 1/8 teaspoon of organic ground clove
- 2 teaspoon of organic vanilla extract

For Topping

- 1 cup of organic raw cacao powder
- 1 cup of organic coconut oil

Directions

1. Take a medium-sized bowl and add all of the listed ingredients under pumpkin filling
2. Mix well until you have a creamy mixture
3. Take another bowl and add the topping mixture and mix well
4. Take a muffin cup and fill it up with 1/3 of the chocolate topping mix
5. Chill for 15 minutes

6. Add 1/3 of the pumpkin mix and layer out on top
7. Chill for 2 hours
8. Repeat until all the mixture has been used up
9. Enjoy!

Nutritional Values per Serving

Calories: 105
Fat: 10.1g
Carbohydrates: 3.3g
Protein: 2.9g

53. Unique Gingerbread Muffins

Serving: 12
Preparation Time: 15 minutes
Cook Time: 30 minutes

Ingredients

- 1 tablespoon of ground flaxseed
- 6 tablespoon of coconut milk
- 1 tablespoon of apple cider vinegar
- ½ a cup of peanut butter
- 2 tablespoon of gingerbread spice blend
- 1 teaspoon of baking powder
- 1 teaspoon of vanilla extract
- 2-3 tablespoon of Swerve

Directions:

1. Pre-heat your oven to a temperature of 350 degrees Fahrenheit
2. Take a bowl and add flaxseeds, sweetener, salt, vanilla, spices and coconut milk
3. Keep it on the side for a while

Dessert

4. Add peanut butter, baking powder and keep mixing until combined well
5. Stir in peanut butter and baking powder
6. Mix well
7. Spoon the mixture into muffin liners
8. Bake for 30 minutes
9. Allow them to cool and enjoy!

Nutritional Values:

Calories:158
Fat: 13g
Carbs: 3g
Protein: 6g

54. The Vegan Pumpkin Spicy Fat Bombs

Serving: 12
Preparation Time: 100 minutes
Cook Time: 0 minutes

Ingredients

- ¾ cup of pumpkin puree
- ¼ cup of hemp seeds
- ½ a cup of coconut oil
- 2 teaspoon of pumpkin pie spice
- 1 teaspoon of vanilla extract
- Liquid Stevia

Directions:

1. Take a blender and add all of the ingredients
2. Blend them well and portion the mixture out into silicon molds
3. Allow them to chill and enjoy!

Vegetarian Cookbook

Nutritional Values:

Calories: 103
Fat: 10g
Carbs: 2g
Protein: 1g

55. The Low Carb "Matcha" Bombs

Serving: 12
Preparation Time: 100 minutes
Cook Time: 0 minutes

Ingredients

- ¾ cup of hemp sees
- ½ a cup of coconut oil
- 2 tablespoon of coconut butter
- 1 teaspoon of matcha powder
- 2 tablespoon of vanilla extract
- ½ a teaspoon of mint extract
- Liquid Stevia

Directions:

1. Take your blender and add hemp seeds, matcha, coconut oil, mint extract and Stevia
2. Blend well and divide the mixture into silicon molds
3. Melt the coconut butter and drizzle them on top of your cups
4. Allow the cups to chill and serve!

Nutritional Values:

Calories: 200
Fat: 20g
Carbs: 3g
Protein: 5g

Dessert

56. The No-Bake Keto Cheese Cake

Serving: 4
Preparation Time: 120 minutes
Cook Time: 0 minutes

Ingredients

For Crust

- 2 tablespoon of ground flaxseed
- 2 tablespoon of desiccated coconut
- 1 teaspoon of cinnamon

For Filling

- 4 ounce of vegan cream cheese
- 1 cup of soaked cashews
- ½ a cup of frozen blueberries
- 2 tablespoon of coconut oil
- 1 tablespoon of lemon juice
- 1 teaspoon of vanilla extract
- Liquid Stevia

Directions:

1. Take a container and mix all of the crust ingredients
2. Mix them well and flatten them at the bottom to prepare the crust
3. Take a blender and mix all of the filling ingredients and blend until smooth
4. Distribute the filling on top of your crust and chill it in your freezer for about 2 hours
5. Enjoy!

Nutritional Values:

Calories: 182

Fat: 16g
Carbs: 6g
Protein: 3g

57. Raspberry Chocolate Cups

Serving: 12
Preparation Time: 60 minutes
Cook Time: 0 minutes

Ingredients

- ½ a cup of cacao butter
- ½ a cup of coconut manna
- 4 tablespoon of powdered coconut milk
- 3 tablespoon of granulated sugar substitute
- 1 teaspoon of vanilla extract
- ¼ cup of dried and crushed frozen raspberries

Directions:

1. Melt cacao butter and add coconut manna
2. Stir in vanilla extract
3. Take another dish and add coconut powder and sugar substitute
4. Stir the coconut mix into the cacao butter, 1 tablespoon at a time, making sure to keep mixing after each addition
5. Add the crushed dried raspberries
6. Mix well and portion it out into muffin tins
7. Chill for 60 minutes and enjoy!

Nutritional Values:

Calories: 158
Fat: 15g
Carbs: 1g
Protein: 3g

58. Exuberant Pumpkin Fudge

Serving: 25
Preparation Time: 120 minutes
Cook Time: 0 minutes

Ingredients

- 1 and a ¾ cup of coconut butter
- 1 cup of pumpkin puree
- 1 teaspoon of ground cinnamon
- ¼ teaspoon of ground nutmeg
- 1 tablespoon of coconut oil

Directions:

1. Take an 8x8 inch square baking pan and line it with aluminum foil to start with
2. Take a spoon of the coconut butter and add into a heated pan; let the butter melt over low heat
3. Toss in the spices and pumpkin and keep stirring it until a grainy texture has formed
4. Pour in the coconut oil and keep stirring it vigorously in order to make sure that everything is combined nicely
5. Scoop up the mixture into the previously prepared baking pan and distribute evenly
6. Place a piece of wax paper over the top of the mixture and press on the upper side to make evenly straighten up the topside
7. Remove the wax paper and throw it away
8. Place the mixture in your fridge and let it cool for about 1-2 hours
9. Take it out and cut it into slices, then eat

Nutritional Values:

Calories: 120
Protein: 1.2g
Fats: 10.7g
Carbs: 4.2g

30-DAY DIET PLAN

DAY	BREAKFAST	LUNCH/DINNER	DESSERT/SNACK
1	Silly Scallion Pancakes	Keto Hummus	White Chocolate Fat Bomb
2	The Keto Crack Slaw	Braised Brussels Sprouts	The Keto Lovers "Magical" Grain Free Granola
3	Feisty Grilled Artichokes	Mexican-Style Dip	Pumpkin Butter Nut Cup
4	The Thundering Cinnamon Chocolate Smoothie	Cheesy Stuffed Peppers	Brownie Balls
5	Squash Salad for the Green Lovers!	Keto Egg Salad	Peanut Butter Fudge
6	Spinach Scramble	Keema Curry	Instant Blueberry Ice Cream
7	Green Eggs	Cheesy Vegetable Dip	Chia Raspberry Pudding
8	Ket-Oats	Savory Cake Bites	Choco Mug Brownie
9	Classic Cheese Soufflés	Roasted Green Beans	Pistachio Ice Cream
10	Vegan Enchilada Macaroni	Spicy Cauliflower Casserole	The Keto Lovers "Magical" Grain Free Granola
11	Quick Breakfast Omelet	Creamy Cauliflower Spinach Soup	Pumpkin Butter Nut Cup
12	Easy and Tasty Egg Scrambl	Brussel Sprout Salad	The Low Carb "Matcha" Bombs
13	Healthy Breakfast Smoothie	Baked Zucchini Eggplant with Cheese	The No-Bake Keto Cheese Cake
14	Almond Coconut Porridge	Creamy Cauliflower Gratin	Raspberry Chocolate Cups
15	The Keto Crack Slaw	Zucchini Hummus	Almond Butter Fudge

16	Vegan Enchilada Macaroni	Spicy Ginger Lime Broccoli	White Chocolate Fat Bomb
17	Squash Salad for the Green Lovers!	Artichoke Dip	No-Bake Raspberry Cheesecake Truffles
18	Feisty Grilled Artichokes		Unique Gingerbread Muffins
19	Green Eggs	Crustless Veggie Quiche	
20	Healthy Breakfast Smoothie	Brussel Sprout Salad	The No-Bake Keto Cheese Cake
21	Green Eggs	Spicy Ginger Lime Broccoli	Choco Mug Brownie
22	The Keto Crack Slaw	Keema Curry	Chia Raspberry Pudding

23	Easy and Tasty Egg Scrambl	Avocado Cilantro Dip	Pistachio Ice Cream
24	Silly Scallion Pancakes	Crispy Broccoli Nuggets	Exuberant Pumpkin Fudge
25	The Thundering Cinnamon Chocolate Smoothie	Healthy Egg Arugula Avocado Salad	Raspberry Chocolate Cups
26	Classic Cheese Soufflés	Fennel Zucchini Pine Nut Salad	The Low Carb "Matcha" Bombs
27	Ket-Oats	Tasty Cauliflower Risotto	The Vegan Pumpkin Spicy Fat Bombs
28	Green Eggs	Coconut Cabbage	Pumpkin Butter Nut Cup
29	Spinach Scramble	Cheesy Baked Zucchini	Strawberry Ricotta
30	Healthy Breakfast Smoothie	Spicy Cauliflower Casserole	Pistachio Ice Cream

CONCLUSION

These recipes are a great way to get started with the vegetarian keto diet. They are not only fun and easy to make, but you will also enjoy them.

Go into this with a full force and reap all the benefits that come with it. Your mind will be in the zone and you will enjoy a healthier lifestyle. Keep in mind that you are not saying "no" to anything, but simply finding ways to enjoy the things that you love without the things that are detrimental to your health.

Wishing you a happy and healthy keto vegetarian lifestyle!

Made in the
USA
Monee, IL